Discussions for Better Relationships

8-Week Group Study Guide based on
The Lost Art of Relationship

✤

DAN CHRYSTAL
WITH JENNIFER EDWARDS

THE SOPHOS GROUP

Discussions for Better Relationships
8-Week Group Study Guide based on *The Lost Art of Relationship*

© 2020 by Dan Chrystal

Published by The Sophos Group, Lincoln, CA 95648. All rights reserved.

For more information about this book and the author, visit www.EveryChurchMatters.com, or www.EveryBusinessMatters.com.

Edited and co-written by Jennifer Edwards, jedwardsediting.net

Interior Design by Linné Garrett, 829Design.com

Cover Design by Susie Aguirre

Cover Photo by Arthur Poulin on Unsplash.com

ISBN: 978-1-7327564-3-4 (print)

ISBN: 978-1-7327564-4-1 (e-book)

Unless otherwise indicated, all Scripture quotations are taken from the Holy Bible, New Living Translation, copyright © 1996, 2004, 2015 by Tyndale House Foundation. Used by permission of Tyndale House Publishers, Inc., Carol Stream, Illinois 60188. All rights reserved.

Where indicated, Scripture quotations are taken from THE HOLY BIBLE, NEW INTERNATIONAL VERSION®, NIV® Copyright © 1973, 1978, 1984, 2011 by Biblica, Inc.® Used by permission. All rights reserved worldwide.

Printed in the United States of America

Dan Chrystal's book, *The Lost Art of Relationship*, is a tremendous blend of inspiration and practical application. You will never view relationships the same way again. As Dan points out, God intended for relationships to be nurtured, treasured and protected. This is one book that is worth your time.

— HAL DONALDSON, PRESIDENT, CONVOY OF HOPE, AUTHOR OF *DISRUPTIVE COMPASSION*

Our churches are packed with people who claim to believe in Jesus...but don't actually do anything he said! This book will make you laugh and cry. It will make you look at things in a fresh new way. And it will definitely make you uncomfortable. Which might be a good thing because ultimately Dan calls us to live, love, and lead like the Jesus we claim to follow.

— RAY JOHNSTON, AUTHOR OF *THE HOPE QUOTIENT* AND
FOUNDING AND LEAD PASTOR AT BAYSIDE CHURCH
ROSEVILLE, CALIFORNIA

Most Christian books are about our most important vertical relationship—us and God—but this book explores what those books don't: the horizontal relationship we are called to as human beings—the relationships we must have with one another. Indeed, this is a lost art that Dan recovers and teaches us about with heart and logic at every turn. I highly recommend it!

— MARK CLARK, AUTHOR OF *THE PROBLEM OF GOD* AND LEAD PASTOR
AT VILLAGE CHURCH SURREY, BRITISH COLUMBIA, CANADA

I still recall the first time Dan came into my office. I couldn't understand why he was so persistent in us meeting. I wondered, what did he want? It didn't take long before I found out...a relationship with me, a stranger whom he only knew by name! He began with wanting to hear my story. I wanted to hand him a copy of my book *Five Years to Life* but decided against it. I then asked him to tell me his story. I don't recall much of it because I never got beyond the story of his father and how he crossed cultural barriers and built relationships lasting over thirty-plus years with individuals that started out as strangers.

This let me know what was "in" Dan. By the time he was done telling me that story I knew we would be brothers. We have had many meetings since that initial one. We have laughed, cried, and ate a lot together...maybe too much! Dan has the gift of risk-taking in seeking out and building relationships. As he writes in this book, step one in building relationships is noticing someone, the last step if you get that far is you become family. If you want a quick fix to relationships, don't read this book. But, if you want to learn how to build life-long, meaningful friendships, then this book might be for you. I would recommend this book not because of Dan's deep research into the subject, but because the subject matter is deeply in him. Dan has made his life's journey living out *The Lost Art of Relationship*.

— DR. SAM HUDDLESTON, ASSISTANT SUPERINTENDENT ASSEMBLIES OF GOD
NORTHERN CALIFORNIA DISTRICT, AND AUTHOR OF *FIVE YEARS TO LIFE*

The Lost Art of Relationship is a fun and fascinating read that reveals stunning insights for loving people and cultivating relationships. It's easy to focus all of our Christian walk on developing relationship with God to the point that we forget to apply God's command in loving others. Loving others is not easy, and sadly, many Christians don't do it well. Dan beautifully illuminates our kingdom mandate while providing brilliant insights, practical steps, engaging stories, and revelations at every turn. Particularly revelatory are the pitfalls and mistakes so many of us make that cost us vibrant and healthy relationships. If you want to fulfill the commandment of loving others (and do it well), this book is must-read.

— ERIC KNOPF, CO-FOUNDER OF WEBCONNEX LLC AND FOUNDER OF EPIC LIFE

What is refreshing about this book is that it not only contains incredible insight and wisdom, but it authentically represents Dan Chrystal. His transparency will undoubtedly touch your heart. I met Dan several years ago at our large church where I served as a pastor. I quickly observed that Dan is one of the most skillful people I have ever met at intentionally developing deep and healthy friendships. Dan is authentic and caring and it shows in the vast number of people who have the blessing of knowing him and their deep affection for him. This book contains the thoughtful wisdom Dan applies to his relationships. I highly and enthusiastically recommend this book as I know anyone who reads and applies it will walk away a better friend, spouse, worker, and person.

— DAN HOUK, PASTOR OF SHADOW MOUNTAIN SOUTH BAY CAMPUS
SAN DIEGO, CALIFORNIA

I heard and, most importantly, have watched Dan Chrystal communicate and live out these principles almost a decade ago. I am so thrilled that he has taken the leap to make these timeless and practical truths available to a larger audience. Not only are you going to enjoy this book, I have a strong hunch that you will never forget it and recommend it to others!

— GAVIN BROWN, SENIOR PASTOR OF LIFEHOUSE CHURCH BELTSVILLE, MARYLAND
WWW.MYLIFEHOUSE.CHURCH

The Lost Art of Relationship is like a road map to finding, building, and treasuring friendships. In spite of all of the "friends" we may have through social media, never before have people seemed so adrift of meaningful, face-to-face relationships. Dan's book provides practical "how-to" advice on finding, building, and valuing close friendships. If you are someone who longs for deeper connections, then Dan's book was written for you!

— CHRIS BUENO, CHIEF EXECUTIVE OFFICER OF OCEAN AVENUE ENTERTAINMENT

Dan and I have lived out the contents of this book through our friendship. I believe Dan's heart for relationships is one of the keys to releasing the kingdom of heaven on earth. My prayer is that everyone who reads this book will be inspired by Dan to become an artist in the golden rule and see God's heart in action.

— DAVE DREVER, FOUNDER AND CHIEF EXECUTIVE OFFICER AT FREELY

Dan Chrystal has written a must-read for anyone considering leading others. His professional personal experiences and knowledge of people make this book a must-read for anyone desiring to build healthy teams and relationships.

— HEIDI HENSLEY, CHILDREN'S PASTOR AT SHADOW MOUNTAIN CHURCH
SAN DIEGO, CALIFORNIA

✣ Contents ✣

&

How to Use This Study

✤

RELATIONSHIPS ARE MESSY.

If you are like me, I need constant reminders to stay focused on others. When writing *The Lost Art of Relationship*, I faced relational challenge after challenge, even in my own family. Whenever I did something wrong, close friends or family members would point out my behavior and rebuke me by saying, "What would your book say?" Ouch! I have been asked multiple times, "What motivated you to write the book?"

Ever since Jesus uttered the words, "'Love your neighbor as yourself'" (Matthew 22:39 NLT), God's enemy has been battling our relationships. Churches do a great job at helping people understand the need and importance of a relationship with God, but when it comes to our relationships with each other...? Well, they come up short.

There are thousands upon thousands of differing denominations, Christian sects, and even more viewpoints about the planet that divide us. There are political factions, which use Scripture to defend their side. There are racial divisions that continue to persist. There are socio-economic divisions that are a constant struggle. And let's get even more personal—family divisions, work issues, friendship issues, marital conflict—the list can go on and on.

Looking back over the last twenty-five years of ministry, it became apparent to me that one message continues to emanate from me. I have a passion deep inside of me that eagerly desires for people to experience the benefits of fulfilling the second most important thing to God—healthy, meaningful relationships with each other.

The feedback I have received from the book has been overwhelming. Many people have requested the book be converted into a small group study. Not only do churches need to focus heavily on helping people to develop healthy relationships, but family members or groups of friends can begin to study relationship essentials and put them into practice at the most foundational level.

With so many issues between people, churches, and denominations (or non-denominations), it is imperative that we begin to introduce healthy conversations into our churches and with each other on how to "love your neighbor as yourself."

Best-selling author Jon Gordon wrote a book *The No Complaining Rule*, where he shares how a front lawn can grow into a healthy, vibrant, green masterpiece. Most people use harsh chemicals, pesticides, weed killer, or pulling to manage the weeds. Here is an excerpt from his book:

> Hope said, "I was wondering how in the world you can eliminate the weeds and prevent them from taking over my lawn without chemicals when everyone in my neighborhood uses chemicals to treat their lawn." "Well, you see, I have a different approach. What I do is treat the lawn with an organic mixture that creates an environment where the good grass can grow healthy and strong. Then it grows and spreads to the point where it crowds out the weeds, and the weeds have nowhere to grow. It's all about the environment. Takes a little longer and a little more work up front, but once you have the good grass growing good and strong, it spreads like kudzu and then you have an amazing, vibrant lawn. Makes everything a whole lot easier, and it's less expensive, too. Instead of spending all that money on chemicals, you simply continue to support a healthy environment." *(Gordon, Jon. The No Complaining Rule (p. 63). Wiley. Kindle Edition.)*

How does this relate to relationships? If we can begin to organically work on them, introducing healthy conversations, healthy perspectives, scriptural foundations, and God-honoring respect, sooner or later the negative relationships will not be able to grow and the good ones will eventually take over.

Unfortunately, Christians have the reputation of being hypocrites. I'll be the first to admit that occasionally I will not react well and my Christian example does not line up with my beliefs. This is the quintessential definition of a hypocrite. However, that mistake makes me a human in need of God's grace and forgiveness. It makes me authentically imperfect. We are imperfect people serving a perfect God.

How about if we turn the reputation around about Christians who are disciples of Jesus? Instead of us telling others what they need to do and not doing it ourselves, let's exemplify to others the love we develop through relationship with each other. Let's make it a priority to bring Jesus's words to life, where He said, "I am praying not only for these disciples but also for all who will believe in me through their message. I pray that they will all be one, just as you and I are one—as you are in me, Father, and I am in you. And may they be in us so that the world will believe you sent me." (John 17:20–21)

This guide is perfect for church small groups or even just a few friends or family members to do together. Over the next eight weeks, you will cover eight relationship essentials, or artforms, including:

- The Art of Forgiveness
- The Art of Encouragement
- The Art of Vulnerability
- The Art of Unity
- The Art of Humility
- The Art of Friendship
- The Art of Community
- The Art of the Question

Each week covers an excerpt from my first book, *The Lost Art of Relationship*, four to five sections of practical questions and relevant Scriptures to look up and discuss, personal application questions to guide your learning, and a guided prayer.

As you walk through this study, may I recommend these few guidelines? Remind your group of these at the start of each meeting.

1. One person should lead the discussion.
2. That leader should set up the question(s) and then be the example and answer it first.
3. Stay on subject.
4. Make sure everyone contributes, no matter how small.
5. Don't be afraid to ask probing questions, and don't settle for simple, one-word answers.
6. Allow five to ten minutes per section, longer if time allows.

I pray that these eight essentials of relationship and the time spent walking through them with your group helps you to grow stronger, healthier relationships throughout your life.

Remember, life is better with great friendships. You're on your way to a great life!

∞

✢ I ✢

The Art of Forgiveness

✣

From the pages of *The Lost Art of Relationship*, page 31:

Have you ever heard the expression, "I forgive you, but I will not forget"? There are still others who say, "If you don't forget, then you have never really forgiven." There are problems with both of these expressions.

For those who say, "I forgive you, but I will not forget," I doubt forgiveness was really given. It sounds like a veiled threat. The next statement, "If you don't forget, then you have never really forgiven," is impossible. You can never really forget what someone has done to hurt you. We were designed to remember. From the day we were born, our brains turn on the memory banks, and we retain massive amounts of information. When we are hurt by someone, or if we hurt someone else, whether intentionally or unintentionally, we remember.

In relationship, two phrases we should focus on more are,

"Please forgive me,"

and

"I forgive you."

This week, we will unpack forgiveness and unforgiveness and the impact each one has on relationships. As you dive into these sections, take a moment to think of an offense you need to forgive someone for (and maybe need to continually forgive), and pray for the Holy Spirit to reveal anything you may need forgiveness for. This lesson may bring up past hurts and issues you haven't thought of in years, so if that is the case for you, I pray for healing, peace, and reconciliation where needed. I hope this lesson is a blessing to you.

———— ♦ ————

1. Relationships are messy. (5-10 minutes)

When you read that sentence, what comes to your mind? Does a circumstance or person pop up in your memory? Do any emotions come into play? Spend a few minutes as a group sharing what "relationships are messy" means to you.

2. We are given two choices regarding forgiveness. (5-10 minutes)

In this world, as soon as sin entered, pain, hurt, offenses, confusion, and disorder entered with it. Whenever someone hurts us, whether intentionally or not, it creates pain, anguish, confusion, feelings of betrayal, and more. It is inevitable that we will hurt others and be hurt.

God gives us *two* legitimate responses to being hurt or offended. We are given a choice to either *not forgive* or *forgive*.

I think we can agree, we have *all* been hurt or offended by someone we know. Maybe someone gossiped about you. Maybe you were physically injured or abused. Maybe someone stole from you. Whatever it was, I'm truly sorry you were hurt. My question is this: Where are you in the forgiveness process regarding this hurt?

3. We are to forgive those who hurt us. (5-10 minutes)

What does the Bible say to do when someone has hurt you? Look up Matthew 18:15–22. What is at the heart of this passage? Who benefits from this instruction?

Of these quotes about forgiveness, which one speaks to your heart and why?

Discuss these with your group.

*"It is one of the greatest gifts you can give yourself,
to forgive. Forgive everybody."*

— Maya Angelou

*"We must develop and maintain the capacity to forgive. He who
is devoid of the power to forgive is devoid of the power to love.
There is some good in the worst of us and some evil in the best of us.
When we discover this, we are less prone to hate our enemies."*

— Martin Luther King, Jr.

*"Darkness cannot drive out darkness; only light can do that.
Hate cannot drive out hate; only love can do that."*

— Martin Luther King, Jr.

Do you believe the phrase, "Forgiveness is a choice"? Talk about it with your group. Is forgiveness something that can just be affirmed in your heart, or does it require action? What kind of action might it require?

4. Choosing to not forgive is also a choice. (5-10 minutes)

Not forgiving someone for something they have done against us is also a choice God gives us as we relate to others. When we do not forgive someone, we are in danger of allowing unforgiveness to fester in our hearts. We are actually in worse shape than the actual damage or pain that was done to us!

In *Lost Art of Relationship*, I describe unforgiveness in terms of bondage, or placing ourselves in a prison cell and giving the person who hurt us the keys to let us out. Take a look at this quote and discuss it with your group. Do you agree or disagree with what it says and why?

*"Unforgiveness chains us to the past, poisons the present,
and keeps us from what the Lord has for our future."*

(Source Unknown)

How does not forgiving someone match up with Scripture? Are there other consequences we experience if we choose not to forgive? Look up Matthew 5:9, 6:15; Romans 12:18; Luke 11:4 to assist with your discussion.

5. When we hurt others, we need to take action. (5-10 minutes)

We would be naïve to think we have never hurt someone, caused emotional pain, or damaged someone. I recognize this takes vulnerability and humility, but our last discussion question will focus inward. If ever we should remember our oath (what is said at our table, stays at our table), now is the time.

Think of a time when you know you caused another person pain or damage. Is there someone God is bringing to your mind, who you might have hurt directly or indirectly?

What does the Bible say to do when we think we might have offended or hurt another person? Read Matthew 5:21–24. What does verse 22 say specifically? If we were to obey this teaching on forgiveness, what might that look like in practical ways? Why do you think Jesus takes this so seriously?

6. Forgiveness is a powerful relationship builder, with God and others. (5-10 minutes)

Forgiveness is not a burden God decided to put on us; it is a tool to build us up, a powerful one. In any relationship, you will need to utilize this tool if you desire to keep, maintain, or grow in your relationships. It can be difficult to forgive—it might even be incredibly uncomfortable and even feel unnatural! But God's desire for us is to be people with deep, meaningful relationships, so He asks us to forgive. He set the example for us in how He forgave us. He forgave us before we even knew we needed it. He offered it to us freely. He even pursues us to let us know that we can live truly forgiven lives.

Read these powerful verses about forgiveness and discuss them as a group.

"If you forgive those who sin against you, your heavenly Father will forgive you. But if you refuse to forgive others, your Father will not forgive your sins."

Matthew 6:14–15

But when you are praying, first forgive anyone you are holding a grudge against, so that your Father in heaven will forgive your sins, too."

Mark 11:25

"If we confess our sins, he is faithful and just and will forgive us our sins and purify us from all unrighteousness."

1 John 1:9

How have you personally witnessed the power of God's forgiveness in either your life or someone else's life? Share this experience with your group. What would it look like if we lived in forgiveness, offering it to others before they hurt us? Is this even possible? I believe it is.

Dear Lord Jesus,

I pray you will help me learn the art of forgiveness in all of my relationships, new and old. Will you help me to know when I have hurt someone, and will you give me the courage and wisdom to reconcile with them to the best of my ability? And for the people who have hurt and offended me in some way (Lord, you know what they are), will you give me your peace, strength, humility, and the ability to forgive them? Not my will, but Your will be done.

Thank you in advance for healing, restoration, unity, and peace in my relationships as I obey you and follow your commands.

In Your Name, I pray,

Amen

✢ **2** ✢

The Art of Encouragement

✤

*"So encourage each other and build each
other up, just as you are already doing."*

(1 Thessalonians 5:11 NLT)

From the pages of *The Lost Art of Relationship*, page 72:

When mastering the art of encouragement, it is so much more meaningful when it comes from someone you have built a relationship with first. Steve's encouragement meant so much more to me because of the relationship he had taken the time to develop with me. Sure, you can encourage someone you barely know. However, the idea here is to understand the importance of the weight your encouragement can carry when you have proven to be a friend through the toughest of circumstances. When you walk *through* the fire with a friend and encourage them in the heat of trouble, your encouragement becomes a lifeline for them.

This is one of the reasons I believe Jesus came to this earth. He walked, talked, lived, and died through life's moments. He understands what it is like to struggle. He walks with us through the most difficult and painful parts of life. His life, death, and resurrection carry so much weight behind them and become the encouragement and hope for our present and future.

As you dive into this week's lesson, I'd like you to think about who needs you to walk with them through the fire of life and struggles of your life. Think of three people who you could encourage today. Who is God calling to your mind to dig deeper into relationship with so you can become a true encourager to them? Write their names down on your paper and pray for them, asking God how He desires you to encourage them.

I hope you find this exercise and discussion to be...well, encouraging!

———————•◆•———————

1. What is true encouragement? What does it take to be a true encourager? (5-10 minutes)

Read these quotes about encouragement and then answer the questions below.

"Gather people around you who are willing to tell you what you don't want to hear."

— Dan Chrystal

"Sometimes, when you're in a dark place you think you've been buried, but actually you've been planted."

— Christine Caine

"Encouragement: When you feel like giving up, remember why you held on so long in the first place."

— Unknown

What does true encouragement mean to you?

Are there any people in your life who have been "true encouragers" to you?

What are some of the qualities those people exhibited to make them "true encouragers"?

THE ART OF ENCOURAGEMENT

2. We all need true encouragers in our life. Do you have one? (5-10 minutes)

When I first started off in the ministry, I learned pretty quickly that Mondays can become a day of discouragement. Why? Think about a great day of ministry on Sunday or the weekend, and then Monday comes. The adrenaline wears off, and it can feel like the world is against you. It was on those days when I sought out friends for encouragement. I still do, for that matter. Proverbs 12:25 is right when it says:

"Worry weighs a person down; an encouraging word cheers a person up."

In your group, talk about a time when you left a discussion with someone who made you feel uplifted, strengthened, with the desire to keep going. What are some other words you could use to describe how they made you feel?

On the flip side, can you think of a time when you left a discussion with someone who made you feel defeated, weak, disheartened, and lost? What did that mean to you? How did you respond? How did it impact your attitude?

3. Perseverance in a relationship impacts our ability to truly encourage others. (5-10 minutes)

True encouragement is most valuable when it comes from a place of trust. Trust is established when we take the time to become friends with someone and develop a meaningful relationship. It requires deciding to stick with the relationship and persevere even when it gets to the point where we may feel, "I don't need this!" Consistency and authenticity are mainstays for true encouragers. If we act one way with one person and another way with others, inconsistency shows our lack of authenticity and that can damage our own reputation. At this point, there is no real relationship, just deception.

There is a verse that is one of my life verses, found in Proverbs 22:1,

"Choose a good reputation over great riches, being held in high esteem is better than silver or gold."

With your group, talk about this idea of perseverance, consistency, and authenticity in relationships.

Has there ever been a time when you felt like giving up on someone? Why?

What about when someone has felt like giving up on you? Why do you think that was?

Who have you pledged to decide to persevere with through most issues?

4. Receiving a rebuke from a friend is actually encouragement. (5-10 minutes)

There is another side to encouragement that most people don't want to talk about... receiving a rebuke or correction. When we receive a rebuke from a friend, it doesn't necessarily feel like encouragement when it happens. There is no question that a true friend has your best interest at heart—they should only want to help you not harm you.

What does the Bible tell us about reproving and rebuking those in Christ who have sinned or are wandering into darkness?

Look up the following verses and discuss with your group.

- 2 Timothy 4:1–3
- Titus 1:12–14
- Galatians 6:1–3
- Ephesians 4:29

How must we handle a reproof or rebuke whether the giver or the receiver of it?

What tone of voice or attitude of heart is needed?

What is at risk if a rebuke is handled incorrectly?

Where do consistency, perseverance, authenticity, and trust come in to play?

5. Proven confidentiality is another mark of a true encourager. (5-10 minutes)

There is one other necessary trait of a true encourager—*proven confidentiality.* The word *confidence* is the feeling or belief that you can truly rely on someone—it takes a firm and established trust.

With your group, discuss the following questions:

How can you determine if you can trust someone to keep something confidential or not?

Why is this a critical element of true encouragement?

How might you train others to become a person who can keep a confidence?

What are some ways you can personally work to keep confidences?

Is there anyone you know who has proven their confidentiality to you?

Dear Lord Jesus,

Truly you are the ultimate encourager in my life. Thank you, Lord, for being willing to carry the weights and burdens of my life in order to give me hope. Lord, I ask that you would encourage_____. They need you so much. Allow me to have the wisdom and courage to come alongside them for the support they need. Open my eyes to see what they truly need, what would be truly helpful. Then, Lord, give me the words, resources, and timing for whatever you need me to do. Help me to be a person who can be trusted to keep a confidence.

Lord, help me to persevere with the difficult people in my life, and please let those who struggle with me to not give up on me either. Help me to be a person who understands sound wisdom from others, allow me to graciously accept it, and prompt me to put it into practice. Thank you for giving me people in my life who truly care about me and want the best for me.

In Your Name I pray,

Amen

✢ 3 ✢

The Art of Vulnerability

✤

"Strength lies in differences, not in similarities."
— Steven Covey

From the pages of *The Lost Art of Relationship* regarding my friendship with Gavin Brown, page 78:

We progressed through the eight stages of relationship and trust became easy for us. Our wives often joked that we had a "bromance," but they knew we had developed a healthy friendship where we were vulnerable with one another. We could shoot straight with each other, be accountable to each other, share our real thoughts without fear of judgment or gossip to others, and support each other through what came to be pivotal moments in our lives…I believe that our vulnerability was the key to growing our relationship, solidifying it for life.

There are other critical lessons I learned about relationships because of Gavin, including being yourself, lessons about color and differences, the need for laughter, staying focused on our passions in whatever ministry we have, and never quit learning.

As you dive into the following questions, think through each one and decide where you are in each of them. How can what you learn about relationships impact others? Where are areas to become more vulnerable, and where are areas that demand more privacy? I hope you find this exercise and discussion to be useful.

------ ◆ ------

1. Vulnerability is a relational tool to be used sometimes and not others. (5-10 minutes)

"If we are not vulnerable, it portrays to others that we don't need them when in fact we need them more than we know."

— Source Unknown

As a group, take time to discuss your experiences with vulnerability. What does it mean to be relationally vulnerable?

Are there areas in life when it isn't wise to be vulnerable? Are there certain people you shouldn't be vulnerable with? How do you know this?

Do you have true vulnerability with any person(s) in your life, including and in addition to your spouse? Are they vulnerable with you?

2. There is extreme value in being yourself. (5-10 minutes)

Insecurity is an epidemic and hits at the core of our true identity. It has the ability to keep us from experiencing solid relationships because we worry about what others might think or feel about us. It keeps us from being vulnerable. Insecurity is also a source of pride, which can look outwardly like arrogance or overconfidence.

"Our insecurities are the inner screams we wish no one would hear."

— Dan Chrystal

Three different times I begged the Lord to take it away. Each time he said, "My grace is all you need. My power works best in weakness." So now I am glad to boast about my weaknesses, so that the power of Christ can work through me. That's why I take pleasure in my

weaknesses, and in the insults, hardships, persecutions, and troubles
that I suffer for Christ. For when I am weak, then I am strong.

(2 Corinthians 12:8–10 NLT)

Spend a few minutes as a group talking about these issues.

Do you suffer from insecurity?

Are there specific areas where your insecurities rise to the surface? Where?

How has insecurity impacted your life and relationships?

What do you think it means to be truly yourself with other people?

Have you experienced this in your life with others?

3. **There are really two antidotes to insecurity that I can think of: the ability to laugh at yourself and intentional vulnerability. (5-10 minutes)**

Do you regularly take time for laughter? How do you achieve this? How can you learn to not take yourself so seriously? Discuss this with your group.

> *"Laughing at yourself and not taking yourself too seriously is an artform. It frees you to be who you really are, own your weaknesses, and enjoy your strengths without becoming arrogant."*
>
> — Dan Chrystal

> *"Intentional vulnerability every day, quiets our insecurities."*
>
> — Dan Chrystal

> *"We cultivate love when we allow our most vulnerable and powerful selves to be deeply seen and known, and when we honor the spiritual connection that grows from that offering with trust, respect, kindness and affection."*
>
> — Brene Brown

The true value of being oneself is the ability to embrace the areas where you are strong and be willing to work on the weaker areas in your life. Discuss with your group ways you can become intentionally vulnerable with someone. What will it require for you to do so? (See James 5:16–17)

4. Differences do and don't matter—let me explain. (5-10 minutes)

Our experiences about where and how we were raised and what we have struggled with have shaped who we are. How we respond to it all and whether or not we are willing to learn things from another person's perspective will determine how we decide to embrace those who "look" different than us. Vulnerability (the opposite of pride) is *required* in order to make this happen.

Discuss these questions with your group:

When it comes to people of different races or color than you, has there been a time when you have worked hard to learn about how they see the world from their perspective?

Are there people of other races and color in your life? Who they are and where did you meet? What kind of relationship have you had with them? What kind of relationship do you hope to have?

What are some of the challenges you have faced and some of the lessons you have learned in having a relationship with people different than you?

5. Never quit learning. (5-10 minutes)

Being vulnerable means to acknowledge you don't know everything and there is a willingness to learn from others. And it requires a certain amount of humility to bring others along in their understanding of things you know about that they don't.

Discuss these questions with your group:

How do vulnerability and our willingness to learn new things coincide?

Are there certain people you can point to who have taught you important lessons in life? Who are they and what have they taught you?

Do you have anyone who is wiser and more experienced than you for learning new things? If you do, who are they? How long have you known them? If not, are there people who come into you mind that you could ask to mentor you?

Do you enjoy learning new things? What kinds of things do you like to learn? How do you best learn new things?

Jesus went straight to the heart of many issues with people laying their vulnerabilities on the table for the purpose of restoration and reconciliation.

Peter after he denied Jesus three times;

The woman at the well;

The woman who was going to be stoned…the list goes on.

May we allow Him to use our vulnerabilities to change us to become more like Him.

Dear Lord Jesus,

Vulnerability can be really difficult, especially when I battle against my own insecurities. I know you say I am your child and that you love me no matter what I do, but sometimes I have a hard time remembering that. I know this belief can get in the way of my relationships and often does, so please help me, Jesus, to walk boldly and confidently in your love, acknowledging that it is okay to mess up sometimes, and it is okay if I don't please everyone. What matters is whether I have pleased you and that requires me being vulnerable to you. It means opening myself up to you and allowing you to speak over and into my life about the areas where I need help. Help me to realize that when I am not vulnerable with you or others, it can actually communicate that I don't need you or others. I know this is the furthest thing from truth.

Thank you for loving me and growing me into a person who is a little more like you every day.

In Your Name I pray,

Amen

✢ 4 ✢

The Art of Unity

✣

From the pages of *The Lost Art of Relationship*, page 90.

With anything that takes effort, discipline (work) is needed to maintain a spirit of unity in relationship. It is one thing to discuss the need for unity; it is another to actually put it into practice. To be disciplined, one needs to become a disciple of Jesus first. Look at Colossians 3:9–11 (NLT).

> *"Don't lie to each other, for you have stripped off your old sinful nature and all its wicked deeds. Put on your new nature, and be renewed as you learn to know your Creator and become like him.*
>
> *In this new life, it doesn't matter if you are a Jew or a Gentile, circumcised or uncircumcised, barbaric, uncivilized, slave, or free. Christ is all that matters, and he lives in all of us."*

Even in the days when Paul wrote to this church in Colossae, people were divided. They were separated into castes, socio-economic status, ethnicity, beliefs, and preferences. Some were even teaching that to believe in Jesus you must be circumcised. Paul blasts that belief into oblivion by stating very simply the sections we have divided ourselves into are of no circumstance in the eyes of God.

This way of thinking was and is so different than how we continue to live our lives, even today. We are still so separated. I would not expect those who do not know Jesus to be forced to adapt to this line of thinking. I would, however, expect those who believe in Jesus and live for Him to understand and live in such a way with other believers that shows we are in complete unity with each other.

Jesus prioritized *unity*. He prayed for *unity*. He desires for us to be in *unity*. This week, we are going to discuss why this principle of unity is essential to relationship. As we do, think about situations and circumstances in your own life where unity has abounded and when it has not. Let's get ready to have a lively and full group discussion.

———————◆———————

1. Jesus expects unity in our worship. (5-10 minutes)

Jesus emphasizes the need for unity among believers many times throughout Scripture. As a group, read the following passages and discuss the questions that follow.

- John 13:34–35
- John 17:20–24

Who is Jesus talking about and what is He saying to them?

What does Jesus say unity or oneness of purpose will accomplish? How does this apply to the way we worship with others who may be in other denominations or different faiths?

Discuss whether or not this is still relevant today or if this is something that was only relevant back in those times. Is it possible to have unity in our differences? Why or why not?

2. It is important to understand what unity really is. (5-10 minutes)

"Unity does not mean sameness. It means oneness of purpose."

— Priscilla Shirer

The dictionary defines unity to be *oneness, sameness, or agreement*. But biblical unity includes oneness of purpose. Not everyone agrees on everything at all times;

I'm not sure that is even possible! Yet Jesus calls believers to be unified.

Discuss your ideas about the following questions with your group.

What do you think Jesus's priorities are in terms of being unified?

What is at stake?

When have you seen unity between relationships or groups?

What did that look like? What impact did it have?

3. Disunity creates division. (5-10 minutes)

Unity is not about everyone agreeing on everything at all times. Yet, disunity feels much like lack of agreement … like when I am driving my wife around. I like to take different routes, and yes, my family jokes that I take the longest route possible to get from point A to point B. We agree on the destination; we just don't agree on how to get there!

Some would see that as *disunity*.

When people are disunified, it means they are divided and disagree so much that they are fighting. There is often much conflict and are separated or divided. This surely isn't Jesus's intention for us, so why does this happen?

Read the following passages and discuss the questions with your group.

- Romans 16:17
- 1 Corinthians 1:10
- Colossians 3:7–15

What are some reasons people disagree or fight?

Why is there so much conflict between people, churches, and groups?

What are you seeing today that is causing disunity?

What do you think is the root cause of disunity?

Who wants people to be divided and separated more than anything else?

When have you seen disunity between relationships or groups?

What did that look like? What impact did it have?

4. Why is unity important for relationships? (5-10 minutes)

"I can do things you cannot, you can do things I cannot; together we can do great things."

— Mother Teresa

We develop bonds as believers to worship, grow, and serve one another in the context of relationship, the places where disciples of Jesus can love their neighbor as themselves and walk in unity with their fellow believers. This is a community where faith comes alive.

As a group, read Acts 4:32–35 and discuss the following questions.

What are some other synonyms of "unity" that you glean from this passage?

How is unity connected to "loving your neighbor as you love yourself"?

Can you share some examples where you have seen similar kinds of unity, cooperation, and community in your life?

I wonder if after reading the Acts passage if some of you instantly thought, *"Well, I wish some of the rich people in here would sell their home and share it with the rest of us."* Still others may have thought, *"Well, that was for then, surely that is not intended for today."*

Both views are the opposite of what we should be thinking. We should be thinking: "What is it that God could be asking me to do in order to show my love for those in the family of God so the world knows that God loves them?"

Will you do this?

5. How can we achieve unity as believers? (5-10 minutes)

"Make every effort to keep yourselves united in the Spirit, binding yourselves together with peace."

— Apostle Paul (Ephesians 4:3 NLT)

Achieving unity requires a commitment to learning how to view people how God sees them. It requires a renewing of your mind away from the "culture-of-me" mindset to one focused on others. When you discipline your mind to see others as God sees them, there is no Jew or Greek, nor black or white or brown, nor male or female, for we are all made in God's image. He is *our* Creator—He created all of us uniquely and by design. And He meant for us to fit together into one body of believers.

Unity is *not* easy. However, it is what Jesus prayed for regarding those who follow Him—and not only us, but anyone who would ever believe in His message. We can pray for opportunities to see the needs of others right around us, and how we can exemplify the love of God in order to show the world around us how much God loves them.

Colossians 3:12–17 literally give us the prescription on how to achieve *unity*. Read these verses together as a group, specifically focusing on 12–17. Now answer the following questions:

Discuss what each of these verses teaches about building unity.

What are some of the key actions or attitudes Paul says promotes unity?

How might you intentionally promote unity in your own life?

Unity lies in the fact that God loves us so much that He sent Jesus to die a criminal's death on the cross. Jesus loves us so much that He was willing to take on our punishment. Our unity is because of Jesus.

Let's pray.

Dear Lord Jesus,

You say in your Word that you are praying for oneness among anyone who will ever believe in you, that your desire for your people is perfect unity. Lord, that is so hard sometimes! We are all so different and we all let pride and our egos get in the way. Sometimes I get caught up in thinking it's more important to be right than remembering you value relationships and friendships more than me being right.

Remind me through your Holy Spirit that unity is far more worthwhile than worrying about differences. Help me to see others through your eyes of unity, oneness, and agreement. Help our world heal and grow towards unity and peace, regardless of our ethnicity, religion, culture, gender, and sexual orientation. You created us all and your will is for all of us to draw near to you in faith, so guide us toward you. Let me be a person who loves others as I love myself, wholly and dearly loved by you.

In Your Name I pray,

Amen

✢ 5 ✢

The Art of Humility

✤

From the pages of *The Lost Art of Relationship*, page 121.

When developing friendships with others, it is incredibly important to remember that just because you are friends does not mean you have permission to rebuke or speak into someone's situation. Ask permission first. This shows humility and respect for the other person.

Humility is about recognizing our place in this world. Andrew Murray wrote a book entitled *Humility*. In this book, he sums up pretty well the lesson on humility and how we should view it:

"Men sometimes speak as if humility and meekness would rob us of what is noble and bold and manlike. O that all would believe that this is the nobility of the kingdom of heaven, that this is the royal spirit that the King of heaven displayed, that this is Godlike, to humble oneself, to become the servant of all."

Loving God helps us to know there is something so much bigger than us. It reminds us that without our Creator, life would not exist. Loving others helps us understand we are not the only one God created. We are each unique and special to Him, sure, but we are not the only ones. Knowing this, we can love others, think of ourselves in sober judgment, and then truly focus on serving other people, especially those in our own community. The question we should ask ourselves is this: "How are we exhibiting humility in our own relationships?" We must recognize our actions do affect others...especially those closest to us.

Humility is unnatural to many of us. We tend to be more about "me" than others. However, Jesus tells us we need to love others as we love ourselves, meaning we are to not consider ourselves better than others. Doing so is the opposite of humility. Instead, we need to consider others in our actions and thoughts. This week, take time to notice tendencies of humility and those opposite of humility, both in yourself and others. Become a student of humility and decide to do as Peter said:

"Clothe yourselves with humility toward one another, because God opposes the proud but shows favor to the humble."

(1 Peter 5:5 NLT)

---◆---

1. Relationship involves the ability to speak and receive truth when warranted. (5-10 minutes)

In relationship, the hope is to get to a place where each person can speak and receive truth in their lives. We all need someone to do this for us at times, but not just anyone is qualified to do so. The ability to speak truth into someone's life requires an established relationship built on trust. It also requires a healthy dose of humility to both give and receive truth. As a group, read the verses below about speaking truth, and discuss the questions that follow.

- Ephesians 4:15
- 1 Corinthians 13:6
- Philippians 2:3

What is the value of speaking truth in another's life? What can it accomplish?

Why is humility needed for giving truth to another person? Why is it important for receiving it? What does this look like?

Can you think of a time when you have had to confront someone about the truth in their life? What about when someone approached you to do the same? Share your experience with the group.

2. Speaking truth to another person requires their emotional consent. (5-10 minutes)

There has to be emotional consent to share concerns or speak into another's life, which comes only by building a solid relationship of trust. And humility is *key* to sharing the truth effectively. Have you ever had a time when you gave your friend your best piece of advice only to find out they didn't want it? This idea of getting permission to speak, before you give advice or your wisdom, gives the other person a chance to decide if they want to hear it or not. Do they want to engage, learn, and grow? Or do they just want to vent, for you to listen and not say anything really useful?

When a person refuses emotional consent, it usually acknowledges they may not be in the right place to hear whatever you have to say at an emotional level. This can save you the heartache of a possible argument or tension in the relationship.

Whenever my wife wants to vent, I love to try to coach her through it. I have a hard time turning that part of me off. However, the best possible question I could ever ask her in that emotional state is, "Would you like me to help you solve this, or do you just want to get it off your mind?"

Requesting emotional consent means to have a mutual understanding and willing agreement between both parties when discussing emotional or potentially emotionally-loaded questions/feedback. Take some time to discuss this idea and these questions with your group.

What comes to mind when you think of "emotional consent" or getting permission to speak into someone's life?

What can happen when we don't have permission to share our feedback?

How can requesting permission strengthen any relationship?

3. Receiving truth from others can be hard, but it's for our good. (5-10 minutes)

It can be difficult to hear feedback from others, but not as difficult when it comes from a friend you trust and have granted permission to speak into your life. It takes implicit trust and humility to speak and receive truth. Some of it will be things you want to hear—other things, not so much.

The Bible has so much wisdom to share with us about humility. Look up the following verses and discuss their application with your group. Answer the questions below.

- Proverbs 11:12
- Proverbs 12:15
- Proverbs 15:31–33

When we are humble, how does it affect our ability to give and receive truth? Are we likely or unlikely to accept the truth? What might our response be without it?

What are some characteristics of a humble person? What is the opposite of humility?

How does a humble attitude heal and calm?

What are ways to strengthen humility in our lives? How can we encourage it in others?

4. Humility in relationship with God. (5-10 minutes)

Humility is defined as a modest or low view of one's own importance. It puts God in His rightful place as Lord and Creator.

Look up the following verses and read what they say about humility. Discuss this with your group.

- Proverbs 22:4
- James 4:6, 10

Along this same vein, Jesus gave this advice to guests at a dinner party:

When Jesus noticed that all who had come to the dinner were trying to sit in the seats of honor near the head of the table, he gave them this advice: "When you are invited to a wedding feast, don't sit in the seat of honor. What if someone who is more distinguished than you has also been invited? The host will come and say, 'Give this person your seat.' Then you will be embarrassed, and you will have to take whatever seat is left at the foot of the table!

Instead, take the lowest place at the foot of the table. Then when your host sees you, he will come and say, 'Friend, we have a better place for you!' Then you will be honored in front of all the other guests.

(Luke 14:6–10 NLT)

You see, Jesus doesn't want us to embarrass ourselves with a self-seeking or prideful attitude. He wants respect and honor and life for us. Let us receive this feedback from Jesus in humility, because,

1) as a believer, you have given Him your emotional consent to speak into your life, and

2) you can trust Him, because He has proven Himself trustworthy. He only has your good in mind.

Do you believe this?

Dear Lord Jesus,

Your Word is so rich with instruction about humility. Jesus, you are the very example of humility in how you came to serve us in our lowly humanity. I acknowledge that humility can be really difficult sometimes, especially when it comes to receiving a truth about myself that I don't necessarily agree with or don't want to hear. Many times, the message of truth is a hidden area of my life that I don't want to face up to, but is necessary for my growth and maturity as a Christian.

Thank you for giving me people in my life, true friends, who will speak courageously and candidly when I need it. Thank you for giving me opportunities to help and encourage others as they give me permission to speak truth into their lives. You left us with many good and wonderful gifts—friends and family who want the best for our lives is one of them.

Teach us to be humble and to resist the temptation for anger and malice and resentment to rule our hearts. Thank you, Jesus.

In Your Name I pray,

Amen

✣ 6 ✣

The Art of Friendship

✣

From the pages of *The Lost Art of Relationship*, page 57,

"A real friend is one who walks in when the rest of the world walks out."
— Walter Winchell

I remember a particularly tough time in my own relational journey. Fortunately, I had a couple of friends who became emotional supports for me. Just knowing they knew what was going on took the pressure off my shoulders. The fact that they walked with me through those dark, emotional moments and didn't leave me to struggle on my own was incredible. They knew just what I needed.

As a student of relationship, it got me thinking about questions such as, what makes a friend? When do we begin to call someone a friend? How do we know we are still friends? Why do we need friends?

These are all excellent questions. One of the best ways for us to have friends is for us to understand, learn, and practice being a good friend. Here, I explain five aspects of a friend that I think will help us with this. When reading through it, though, try not to think about how *someone else* needs to hear this.

NOTES

These five aspects of a friend were taught and modeled to me by one of the greatest friends someone can have. They describe who a friend should be, what a friend should do, and how a friend should act. I mentioned before that I think we rush into calling people "friend" without truly understanding the implications of what it means to be someone's true friend. I hope this chapter will clarify this and help you as you continue to develop healthy friendships throughout your life.

Before we begin this week, I would like us to think about the people we would call "friend." You may have many so-called "friends," but are they really your friend? How can you know? How can you know if you are being a good friend to others? There is much to be gained if we can get this right.

This week, we will delve into the five aspects of a friend. When you consider your friendships, think about each person through this lens. We also need to think about how we stack up as someone's friend. How well are we doing in each of the five aspects? Let's get ready to have a lively and full group discussion.

———————◆———————

1. A friend *connects* and *shares life* with you. (5-10 minutes)

True friendships require connection. Connection is not just "chemistry," where we instantly get along. Connection is much stronger. It is literally sharing "life." Connection takes intentionality, time, and emotional investment.

There are four reasons for connecting with others:

1. It benefits me.
2. It benefits you.
3. It should benefit others.
4. It pleases God.

These are the basis for friendship.

Look up and read the following verses and discuss the questions with your group:

- 1 Thessalonians 2:8
- James 5:16
- Luke 6:31

What does each verse say about friendship? What traits do they explore?

What kinds of things are we meant to share with others?

How can connection take place in friendships?

What obstacles get in the way of connecting and sharing life with other people?

What stops you from connecting with others?

2. A friend shows *emotion* on your behalf and is moved to action. (5-10 minutes)

Compassion is having a deep awareness of the suffering of another living being accompanied by a desire to bring relief. Compassion is quite literally, *Love in Action*. Love is a behavior, an action, a decision. Add to that the emotional connection and you are driven to the aid of someone. Compassion is not an emotion on its own; it requires action. When you recognize the hurt, pain, sickness, or sadness of someone else and you *do* something about it, you demonstrate compassion. This is a crucial connection point that deepens a friendship.

As a group, read Romans 12:15 and discuss the following questions:

Discuss a time when you have demonstrated compassion for another person, or if you have been the recipient of compassion from another.

How can righteous anger be used for a friendship? What might that look like?

What about happiness and grief?

In light of Romans 12:15, what is your role in relationship?

3. A friend *sticks with you,* especially when the going gets tough. (5-10 minutes)

> *"Fake friends are like shadows. They follow you in the sun but leave you in the dark."*
>
> — Source unknown

We all go through dark times; it is inevitable in this world. But true friends have a part to play in our struggles. Look up the verses below, and discuss the questions that follow with your group.

- Proverbs 18:24
- Job 2:11
- Ecclesiastes 4:9–10
- Galatians 6:2

Think of such a time when what you were going through seemed unbearable.

Who was there with you?

Who stuck with you even though it may have been difficult for them?

Are there two or three people in your mind who fit this description?

Were there any people mysteriously absent?

Who would you call on if you found yourself in a difficult season?

4. A friend *tells the truth;* they won't just watch you fail. (5-10 minutes)

We learned last week about giving truthful feedback to people in our lives. Sometimes we are faced with a situation where we have to tell someone the cold, hard truth. God uses us to rebuke others when we see them going down the wrong path, or are about to do harm to their lives or someone else's. But there is a way to go about it.

Read the verses below and then discuss their applications with your group. Answer the questions that follow.

- "As iron sharpens iron, so one person sharpens another." (Proverbs 27:17 NLT)

- "Wounds from a friend can be trusted, but an enemy multiplies kisses." (Proverbs 27:6 NLT)

- "Perfume and incense bring joy to the heart, and the pleasantness of a friend springs from their heartfelt advice." (Proverbs 27:9 NLT)

- "Instead, we will speak the truth in love, growing in every way more and more like Christ, who is the head of his body, the church." (Ephesians 4:15 NLT)

With your group, talk about any experiences where you either had to tell someone the hard truth, or you were the receiver of some hard truth. What kind of an impact did that experience have on the person (or you)? Did it strengthen or damage the friendship?

What does Ephesians 4:15 say about what our heart attitude should be for truth-telling, and what is the end-goal? Who does it benefit?

5. A friend will *sacrifice* for you. (5-10 minutes)

God calls each one of us to sacrifice for the sake of others, especially those we consider our friends.

Look up the following verses, and discuss their application with your group.

- John 15:12–13
- John 13:34–35

What kind of sacrifices can we make for others? Brainstorm some sacrificial options.

Is the Holy Spirit bringing anyone to your mind who needs your sacrifice? What is He telling you?

What happens when the world sees people connecting, rejoicing, loving, and sacrificing for one another?

What we feel and do for our friends has an impact on those around us. It is up to us to influence others positively. Take this challenge today: practice all five of these aspects with the friendships you already have in your life, then begin to show them to people who are not yet your friend. See how your connection and actions can become a catalyst for life-change in someone else's life. Are you up for the challenge?

Let's pray.

Dear Lord Jesus,

You are our ultimate friend. You set the best example for us of what a true friend is like. You connect with us personally; you spend time with us; you are there in our rejoicing and mourning; you tell us the truth knowing it will set us free. And most of all, Jesus, you sacrificed it all for us—you lay down your very life for us so we can be free from sin and death, and also spend eternity with you.

Lord Jesus, help us to become your kind of friend for others. Help us to strengthen the areas where we are weak and use the areas where we are strong. Bring to our minds someone who needs a new friend, someone who needs to know the truth about you, someone we can serve on your behalf.

In Your Name I pray,

Amen

* 7 *

The Art of Community

✣

"Why build community with others? Because we could be one relationship away from changing the course of our destiny."

— Dan Chrystal

From the pages of *The Lost Art of Relationship*, page 145.

Don't underestimate the effectiveness and power of expanding your community of friends and connections. All it takes is some time, intentionality, asking some good questions, a listening ear, and allowing yourself to know others and be known by them. From this, you will be surprised at how the hand of God is working, even though it might take time.

Building a community is more than just making an infinite number of connections. It is being an influence for Christ in as many arenas as possible, which gives you more opportunity to be an extension of God's hand in this world.

Plant seeds of relationship. Be patient. Nurture these relationships and stay connected to the ones you have always had. Pray and trust God to work through them.

The Art of Community is concerned about meeting needs and connecting people who can help each other. In other words, it is a tool we can use to love our neighbor as ourselves (Matthew 22:39). This is our focus this week.

"There is no power for change greater than a community discovering what it cares about."

— Margaret J. Wheatley

"The greatness of a community is most accurately measured by the compassionate actions of its members."

— Corretta Scott King

———— ♦ ————

1. The Meaning of True Community (5-10 minutes)

"Networking is rubbish; have friends instead."

— Steve Winwood, Music Artist

Networking has become a "buzz" word; however, the art of community is something different. Networking is based on needing something from someone, sort of a "I'll-scratch-your-back, if-you-scratch-mine" mentality, whereas building community is mutual and inclusive. The difference between the two is huge in terms of relationship.

Here is one definition of community:

A **community** is a group of people who share something in common. You can **define a community** by the shared attributes of the people in it and/or by the strength of the connections among them. You need a bunch of people who are alike in some way, who feel some sense of belonging or interpersonal connection. (www.artofrelevance. org, 2/20/18)

How do you define community?

What is the purpose of community? How does it benefit people?

What are some obstacles to building community?

2. The Bible and Community (5-10 minutes)

God made each of us for community and He tells us what community should look like in His Word. Acts 4:32 says, "All the believers were united in heart and mind. And they all *felt* that what they owned was not their own, so they shared everything they had."

The key phrase here is: *"united in heart and mind."* There's unity again! In the case of the first-century believers, they had a common connection and a common threat to their existence. Jesus had been crucified, raised, and ascended to His Father. The disciples had been in hiding and now the Holy Spirit had been poured out on them, and thousands came to know Christ in a matter of weeks.

They also had a mission. They prayed for boldness in preaching God's Word, to be evidenced in healings that would take place, and miraculous signs and wonders through the name of Jesus. Because of this message, they were united in heart and mind with one goal—preach the word of God with boldness.

This bound them together and they were able to move and operate as a community, and this drove them to share what they had to complete that mission and goal.

With your group, look up the following verses and discuss the following questions.

- Matthew 18:19–20

- Hebrews 10:23–25

- Romans 12:9–16

What do these verses say about community and how God views their functionality?

What do they say about their purpose?

How are we to treat one another in community?

What is God calling your community to do and share?

3. Developing and Expanding Community (5-10 minutes)

"There is no power for change greater than a community discovering what it cares about."

— Margaret J. Wheatley

Communities have to be built, which requires time, intentionality, and trusting God with opportunities. Community building might come about with a simple nudge from the Holy Spirit inspiring you to connect with someone specific. Or maybe a connection made organically at a coffee shop or your workplace. Sometimes other people are involved, introducing us to one of their connections. Either way, there is value in every connection we make.

Discuss the following questions with your group thinking about your own experiences in building community.

How do you typically build community?

Do you have a best practice in connecting with others?

Are there things you could be doing to build community that you're not doing?

4. Examining Our Own Communities. Is There Room for More? (5-10 minutes)

"One of the most important things you can do on this earth is to let people know they are not alone."

— Shannon L. Alder

We all have a community, whether big or small. There are times in life when we feel hungry for community, and gathering people around us comes easily. And sometimes we can be satisfied with the "us-four-and-no-more" mentality, or we limit who we do relationship with based on similarities, locale, or circumstance. I fully believe there are people out there who need a community, who are waiting and hoping for people to connect with. And sometimes those folks don't look like us, talk like us, or think the same way we do.

When we connect with others, God will use us and those within our community to benefit the greater community. This enhances the relationships within the community, and eventually influences those who will become a part of that greater community simply because we were willing to reach out beyond what we thought we were capable of.

Discuss the following questions with your group.

Can you describe a time when you connected with another person because of the prompting of the Holy Spirit? You might think of it as a "divine appointment."

Is there anyone in your community who needs to know someone else in your community? Is there someone who comes to mind who needs connection?

Does a specific need of one community member come to mind that maybe you or someone else in your community can help with?

Who has been the most surprising connection for you so far in life?

Dear Lord Jesus,

We were made for community. You know what is best for us. You love us.

Thank you that we are not all a bunch of hermits, restless wanderers who live alone, only caring for ourselves. You know that sharing and encouraging, supporting and meeting needs is for more than the people we help. It's for us as well. Help us to grow into full maturity of faith and your likeness.

Help us, Holy Spirit, to be mindful of anyone in our lives we aren't seeing clearly, who needs our connection or for us to connect them with someone else. Prompt us and give us clarity with a will to obey your holy nudges. Give us courage to reach out, and bless those relationships when we do. You know each and every one of us and what we all need. Thank you for caring for us through community.

In Your Name I pray,

Amen

* 8 *

The Art of the Question

From the pages of *The Lost Art of Relationship*, page 182.

We should never underestimate the *power* of the question in relationship. Questions are so much better than assumptions or even statements. Making a statement into someone's life can hurt, be off-target, and cause damage. Asking questions, especially when said in context and with sincerity, have a way of opening up a relationship. It shows you are interested in the other person. It shows you have genuine concern for them, and you do not necessarily know the answer. It shows you are willing to walk through a life circumstance, discover, learn, and grow together.

Questions have a way of taking a shallow conversation into a deep-water dive where you can find answers you have always been looking for but could never see at the surface. As long as questions are present, relationships can continue to grow and develop. When questions cease in a relationship, it is only a matter of time before a separation begins to take place. We replace the questions with assumptions, implications, and doubt.

"The first step to receiving an answer is being brave enough to ask a question."
—Kaitlyn Bouchillon

In relationship, asking questions can become a catalyst for helping us and others stretch beyond our comfort zones, expand our community of friends, provoke new experiences, and enrich our lives. The Art of the Question is a powerful tool. When coupled with listening, artful questions have the ability to deepen and authenticate relationships like nothing else.

This week, we are going to break up into groups of two. Choose someone you may not know as well as the others. If you're doing this study on your own, you can talk to your spouse, a friend, or someone you're just getting to know. Try it! I think you'll see how carefully-formed questions can open doors to true relationship.

———— ◆ ————

1. Ask questions to get better understanding. (10 minutes)

"Questions are the doorbells to relationship.
Ask the right ones, and someone might let you in."

— Dan Chrystal, *The Lost Art of Relationship*

How many times have you offered an opinion without first seeking information? I have, and let me tell you, it has gotten me into trouble. Without asking questions, how are we supposed to know what or who we're dealing with? We can easily misjudge a situation or person, or miscalculate their motives and intentions about why they do the things they do.

Whenever I meet anyone for the first time, I have a list of questions to ask so I can get to the know the person and their history—their *story*. My point is to understand *why* someone makes the choices they do in life rather than just *what* they do. The *why* behind things is very important—they give you important insight into what makes that person tick.

The very first questions I ask are:

Where were you born?

How did you get to where you are right now?

I will ask them to fill in as much information as they want, but let them know that I may stop them along the way to ask questions raised with the information they give.

With your partner, take five minutes each to ask and answer the above two questions. Listen and take note of the details of their story. Write them down if need be.

2. Ask probing and get-to-know-you questions to dig deeper. (10 minutes)

"Unanswered questions are not threats; they are challenges and catalysts."

— Colin Wright

"No one can know a person's thoughts except that person's own spirit, and no one can know God's thoughts except God's own Spirit."

(1 Corinthians 2:11 NLT)

You have experienced it, and you have probably done it yourself: you ask someone you know, "How are you doing?" Their answer? "Fine."

Most people will not offer anything more than that response. But using active listening allows us to formulate direct or probing questions that makes them think. When I am continuing to get to know someone, I ask questions like,

What is the best thing that has happened to you this past week?

Is there something you are really looking forward to or planning in your life?

Is there something or someone in your life weighing you down that I can pray for?

These types of questions should leave room for the person to decide how much to share and what to share. They are more meaningful than just asking how they are doing. These are non-threatening, and you'll really start getting to know someone more deeply as they open up and share with you. Often, they will return the same question in response, so make sure you have thought your answers through!

With your partner, spend five minutes each asking a few direct or probing questions from the information you discovered from the first discussion. Be creative, and remember to allow permission to not answer if one of you isn't comfortable doing so.

3. Ask questions to help resolve conflict. (10 minutes)

"Most misunderstandings in the world could be avoided if people would simply take the time to ask, 'What else could this mean?'"

—Shannon L. Alder

"Search for the Lord and for his strength; continually seek Him."

(Psalm 105:4 NLT)

Let's face it. Sin and pride get between people. We hold our possessions in higher regard than our relationships sometimes. We tend to consider ourselves first, which definitely hinders relationship. We can over-analyze someone else's behavior or words until we have embellished the story in our minds. Conflict is bound to happen in this fallen world.

Questions can open the window so you can air out grievances and get a better understanding of the conflict, but *not* questions like these:

Why are you such an idiot?

What is wrong with you!?

Why can't you understand your problem?

In any conflict, we would be wise to take a moment to settle our emotions and objectively think through what is going on before asking any questions. Then the questions we may wish to ask should help get to the heart of the issue, like the following,

Okay, so this is what I heard or felt. Is this what you meant?

Would you help me understand... (fill in the blank with the issue)

Is there something I said or did that may have caused you to be hurt or offended? (Warning: This last question is tricky...If you are not prepared to hear the answer, then don't ask it.)

These kinds of questions help us process through a conflict, and if you are receptive to the answers, they can help to resolve the conflict and even draw you closer to the person you have the conflict with. Of course, you cannot guarantee this, but you will know you did what was necessary to try and reconcile things.

With your partner,

Talk about how you can resolve conflicts with other people.

What have you found to work and doesn't work?

Share your best practices with each other.

4. Ask questions to lead others to Christ. (10 minutes)

The disciples learned that a relationship with God involves questions. They asked questions all the time of Jesus! And Jesus was always asking them questions. One such time is recorded in Matthew 16:13–20.

Jesus and his disciples had arrived in Caesarea Philippi, and while they were spending some time together, Jesus decided to ask them a question about who others believe him to be. The murmur of the crowds had entered their ears, and they responded by saying, "Some say John the Baptist, some say Elijah, and others say Jeremiah or one of the other prophets."

This was just a precursor question, because then Jesus asked them directly, "But who do you say I am?" This direct, probing question brought the disciples to the doorway of faith. If they made this confession of faith about who Jesus really is, they could walk through the door to a deeper relationship with Him!

With your partner, spend the next ten minutes on these four points:

Look up Matthew 6:13–20 and read the rest of the story.

Discuss the implications between this question and the role relationship played in the answer.

How deep are you allowing your relationships to go?

Are you building up the faith of others with your questions? How so?

"Keep on asking, and you will receive what you ask for. Keep on seeking, and you will find. Keep on knocking, and the door will be opened to you."

(Matthew 7:7 NLT)

Questions are the shovels that help us dig deeper into relationship. You may be afraid of what someone might uncover that has been buried for a long time. However, the more we expose ourselves to those we trust, the deeper we can go, and the more meaningful our relationships can become. Without probing questions, our relationships will only stay on the surface.

We should always be on the quest for discovery about the people in our lives. Questions help us on our journey to discover the lost art of relationship. My philosophy rests on the fact that if I treat people how I want to be treated, I will ask them about their life. I will ask probing questions. I will never stop asking questions. Because sometimes, questions open the door to a relationship, even with Christ.

Next time you meet someone, ask them to coffee and ask the two questions:

Where were you born?

How did you get to where you are right now?

Then listen to their story, cuing in to certain details. You can learn a lot about someone by actively listening to their story. The moment you stop asking questions in your relationships, that is the moment your relationships stop growing.

Dear Lord Jesus,

Thank you for giving us curiosity about others and their lives. You modeled how questions can lead to relationship and the doorway to faith in you. Help us to practice this art of the question in all of our relationships. Give us an ear to listen actively and help us to form healthy, probing, life-giving questions that lead to deeper relationships, especially one with you.

May we never cease to ask questions in our relationships and in our relationship with you. May we keep on seeking, keep on asking, and keep on knocking, as we desire to grow in our knowledge and relationship with you and then take that into all of our other relationships.

In Your Name I pray,

Amen

✣ About Dan Chrystal & The Sophos Group ✣

✤

Dan Chrystal is an avid student of relationship. With over twenty-five years of ministry and relationship experience, Dan serves as one of the pastors at Bayside Church under the dynamic leadership of founding pastor, Ray Johnston. He is on Bayside's Thrive leadership team, a growing conference that reaches thousands of leaders every year, where he oversees sponsorship acquisition and national church relationships.

Dan is a vibrant speaker and a dedicated life, career, and couple's coach. He is the owner of The Sophos Group, a coaching and consulting firm, and he also oversees the business side of his wife's corporation. He holds an MBA in executive leadership from Kaplan University (now Purdue Global University) and is currently studying law at Concord Law School.

His extensive ministry background has taken him all over the country, and he has served in varying capacities, including Lead Pastor, Administrative Pastor, Associate Pastor, Worship Leader, and Youth Pastor. He has lived in Baltimore, near Philadelphia, inner-city New Jersey, Central Coast California, Los Angeles, and now Northern California. In each place, Dan has developed deep and meaningful relationships with many people.

A champion for connecting people, relationships are at the core of who he is. It is not uncommon to find him spending time with others at coffee shops, restaurants, offices, or at his home getting to know as many people as his schedule allows.

His passion, mission, and purpose are to pass along what he has learned about relationship from key people in his life, helping others understand and put into practice what "loving their neighbors as themselves" truly means.

Dan and his wife, Tania, live in Lincoln, California. Together they have two daughters, two grandchildren, three dogs, and a full life! His first book, *The Lost Art of Relationship*, is available at Barnes & Noble.com, Amazon.com, and Christianbook.com. Connect with Dan through email at thesophosgroup@gmail.com.

"Choose a good reputation over great riches."

Proverbs 22:1

❖

✤ About Jennifer Edwards ✤

✤

Jennifer Edwards is a professional editor, writer, and publishing coach serving Christian authors and publishers. She has worked with over thirty authors and numerous Christian publishers over the past nine years, including Faithlife/Lexham Press, Principles to Live By Publishing, BMH Books, Compel/She Speaks authors, Redemption Press, Gospel Advocate, The Sophos Group, and more.

Her master's degree in Biblical and Theological Studies from Western Seminary has proven invaluable in helping Christian authors with their manuscripts by providing a critical eye for content, a thorough understanding of Scripture, and insightful, theological thinking.

Jennifer has co-authored two books, *Discussions for Better Relationships* study guide and *God's Radical Plan for Wives* by Gil and Dana Stieglitz. She authored the companion study guide for that book as well.

To contact Jennifer, email her at mail.jennifer.edwards@gmail.com.

Or visit www.jedwardsediting.net.

Relationships Are Beautiful Messes

★★★★★

RELATIONSHIP IS A JOURNEY OF DISCOVERY—a lost art. In this generation, it has become challenging to deepen and grow personal relationships with each other. Our technology-flooded environment has left many with limited relational experience and a fear of face-to-face connection and meeting new people.

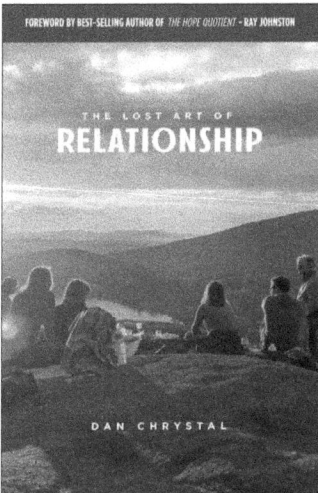

The Church has done a decent job of helping people understand the need and importance of a relationship with God, but what about with each other? At the heart of every man, woman, and child is the need for connection—for relationships with people who love them for who they are.

In the *Lost Art of Relationship*, Dan Chrystal tackles the heart of relationship based on the time-honored instruction to "love your neighbor as you love yourself." But what does that mean? How do we live out this odd instruction? Who is my neighbor, anyway? What makes relationships healthy, and what makes them fail? Through Dan's personal stories and difficult life lessons, you will come away encouraged, inspired, and motivated to love those in your life more fully. If you desire deep and meaningful connections, now is the time to discover the *Lost Art of Relationship*.